IMAGES
of England

PARNALL'S
AIRCRAFT

Parnall Puffin two-seat fighter-reconnaissance seaplane with wings folded at the Isle of Grain Royal Naval Air Station, *c.* 1920-21.

IMAGES
of England

PARNALL'S AIRCRAFT

Compiled by
Ken Wixey

TEMPUS

First published 1998
Copyright © Ken Wixey, 1998

Tempus Publishing Limited
The Mill, Brimscombe Port,
Stroud, Gloucestershire, GL5 2QG

ISBN 0 7524 1508 5

Typesetting and origination by
Tempus Publishing Limited
Printed in Great Britain by
Midway Clark Printing, Wiltshire

To my wife Jean

Parnall Type 382 and its slotted wing, installed here for the first time on an elementary trainer.

Contents

Introduction   7

1.   Parnall & Sons Ltd   9

2.   Fishponds, The War and Beyond   25

3.   George Parnall & Co., 1920-1935   41

4.   Sub-Contracts   81

5.   Parnall Aircraft Ltd, 1935-1946   97

Acknowledgements   128

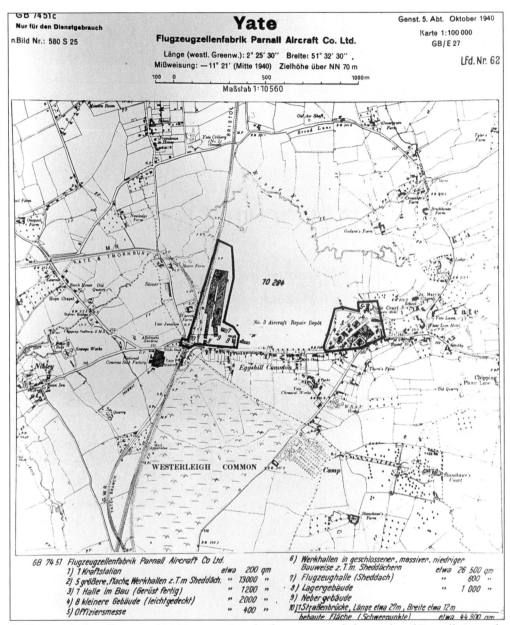

Yate

Flugzeugzellenfabrik Parnall Aircraft Co. Ltd.

Länge (westl. Greenw.): 2° 25′ 30″   Breite: 51° 32′ 30″ .
Mißweisung: —11° 21′ (Mitte 1940)   Zielhöhe über NN 70 m

100   0   500   1000 m
Maßstab 1:10560

GB 74 51 Flugzeugzellenfabrik Parnall Aircraft Co Ltd.
  1) 1 Kraftstation   etwa 200 qm
  2) 5 größere, flache, Werkhallen z.T.m Sheddäch.   " 13000 "
  3) 1 Halle im Bau (Gerüst fertig)   "   1200 "
  4) 8 kleinere Gebäude (leicht gedeckt)   "   2000 "
  5) Offiziersmesse   "   400 "

  6) Werkhallen in geschlossener, massiver, niedriger
     Bauweise z.T.m. Sheddächern   etwa 26 500 qm
  7) Flugzeughalle (Sheddach)   "   800 "
  8) Lagergebäude   "   1000 "
  9) Neber gebäude
 10) 1Straßenbrücke, Länge etwa 27m, Breite etwa 12m
     bebaute Fläche (Schwerpunkte)   etwa 44 900 qm

A German Luftwaffe map of 1940 portraying the layout around the works of Parnall Aircraft, which are to the left of centre.

6

Introduction

A Triad of Companies

After setting up shop in 1820 at Narrow Wine Street, Bristol, one William Parnall began trading as a weights and measures manufacturer. Later the firm was established as Parnall & Sons Ltd, renowned for its expertise in cabinet making, fabrication of shop fronts, shopfitting and associated equipment. The fine range of weighing and measuring machines drew the attention of W. & T. Avery, a well-known producer of weights, measures and weighing requisites. Avery's came to a satisfactory financial settlement with Parnall, taking over the manufacture of Parnall-designed weighing apparatus. However, for trading purposes the name of Parnall & Sons Ltd was retained.

At the outbreak of the First World War in August 1914, the managing director of Parnall & Sons Ltd was George Geach Parnall, who had developed the family business further, their expertise in woodcraft being well known. This prompted a request for Parnall & Sons Ltd to manufacture wooden aeroplanes for the British Admiralty, including Avro 504s, Sopwith (Fairey) Hamble seaplanes and land planes, Short seaplanes and Short bombers. In addition, the company produced a one-off single-seat Scout (Zepp Chaser) and the Panther two-seat naval spotter reconnaissance biplane, which reached production status.

This influx of aviation work necessitated the acquisition of additional premises, sites being taken over at the Coliseum, Park Row, Bristol, Eastville (Mivart Street), Brislington and at Quakers Friars. Developed at Brislington, the Panther was designed by Harold Bolas, loaned as an aircraft designer in 1917 to Parnall by the Admiralty. He stayed on with the company and, after George Parnall disagreed with Avery's over their views on further aviation work, joined George Parnall when he formed his own company named George Parnall & Co.

Avery moved from Narrow Wine Street to Lodge Causeway, Fishponds, where a site had been vacated by Cosmos Engineering in 1919. They had built aero-engines, including the Cosmos Jupiter designed by Roy Fedden (later Sir Roy), and when the company went into voluntary liquidation, the newly formed aero-engine division of the Bristol Aeroplane Co. took them over, acquiring five Jupiter engines (later improved to become the famous Bristol Jupiter), the services of Roy Fedden (later Sir Roy) and most of Cosmos' experienced staff.

Meanwhile, at Fishponds Parnall & Sons Ltd faced stiff opposition from George Parnall & Co., and in 1932 Avery purchased outright their rival's shopfitting business. This left the way clear for George Parnall to concentrate more on his aviation interests. But Parnall & Sons Ltd themselves became involved again in wooden aircraft construction, starting in 1939. Orders flowed in for de Havilland (DH) Tiger Moth airframes, wings for Airspeed Oxfords and, later, components for carrier-borne Fairey Barracuda torpedo/dive-bombers, Short Stirling fins, Handley Page Halifax wing flaps, Bristol Beaufighter tailplanes and numerous parts for DH Mosquitoes. Many fuselages were also produced for the Airspeed Horsa, a large troop-carrying glider used during Allied landings in France and at Arnhem.

After the Second World War, Parnall's at Fishponds fabricated metal components for the aircraft industry which included fuselage sections for DH Venom jet fighters, tailplanes for DH Herons and wing ribs for DH Doves. Fittings and components were also produced for the Bristol 170 Freighter, Britannia turboprop airliner, DH Comet jet airliner and Hawker Siddeley HS 125 executive jet. Interior items were also built for the mock-up and prototype of the Concorde supersonic airliner.

Meanwhile, following the First World War, George Parnall & Co. built their first early aircraft alongside the cabinet making shop at the Coliseum works, Harold Bolas following his Panther design with the Puffin naval amphibian and Plover single-seat naval fighter. The Puffin was test-flown from the Isle of Grain Naval Air Station, but other early Parnall machines flew from Filton under an arrangement with Bristol Aeroplane Co. until George Parnall & Co. moved to Yate.

The transfer to Yate, Gloucestershire (now in Avon), nine miles from Bristol, was ideal for George Parnall & Co. It was the site of an old RFC/RAF aerodrome, with office block, works and a design office. The snag was a limited take-off run of 1,500ft into a prevailing wind, with pilots having to climb over works, hangars, a main railway line, rail sidings and some houses. But it did mean the company could design, construct and test-fly its aircraft at a single place.

Harold Bolas produced a varied mixture of military and civil aircraft types for George Parnall & Co., with names like Pixie, Perch, Pike, Peto, Pipit, Prawn, Parasol, Imp and Elf. He also studied a 'bodyless' monoplane layout in which a flying-wing, incorporated into a very wide fuselage, produced a continuous aerofoil section for both the wing and body. Although a clever theory, this design proved disappointing in wind-tunnel tests and was abandoned. Bolas left Parnall's for America in 1929, where he became a partner in the Crouch-Bolas Aircraft Company.

Most Parnall-designed aircraft were prototypes or experimental machines, and by 1932 George Parnall was selling off a number of assets; the top works at Yate went to Newman's electric engineers and, as mentioned earlier, his Bristol-based shopfitting business was sold to his old rival Avery's. By 1935 the RAF was expanding fast and, as only one Parnall G.4/31 general purpose biplane (already obsolete) was nearing completion, George Parnall sold the remaining Yate site and retired. He continued living in Bristol, but sadly died on 21 June 1936, after suffering a cerebral haemorrhage. He was buried in the parish churchyard at St Gennys in his native Cornwall.

Meanwhile the Yate site was acquired by Nash & Thompson Ltd (later Parnall Aircraft Ltd), noted for its power-operated aircraft gun turrets. The Hawker Demon two-seat fighter was fitted with their 'lobster-back' turret in the rear cockpit and, as a European war loomed nearer, orders began to flow in to Parnall Aircraft Ltd for Frazer-Nash turrets as equipment for RAF Whitley and Wellington bombers, Blackburn Bothas (then a promising torpedo-bomber) and Short Sunderland flying boats.

On the afternoon of 27 February 1941, a lone German Heinkel He 111 bomber bombed the Yate works and over fifty employees were killed, many injured and considerable damage caused to the factory. On 7 March a repeat raid was carried out, again by a single Heinkel, and although casualties were lower, material damage was more serious. Production halted temporarily, but eight days later started again at a satellite factory in Dursley. Several other sites around Gloucestershire and Bristol were used by Parnall's during the war, but most impressive was the large modern works rebuilt on the site of the old bombed-out Yate factory. Parnall's Aircraft was in full production there well before the war ended, building nose and tail turrets for Lancaster bombers, Spitfire airframes, components for Lincoln bombers and, later, parts for Gloster Meteor jet fighters. This factory employed 3,500 people, but immediately after the war

One
Parnall & Sons Ltd

One of eight Short 827 seaplanes, produced by Parnall & Sons Ltd, nears completion at the Coliseum works, Bristol, *c.* 1915. The engine fitted was a 150hp Sunbeam Nubian.

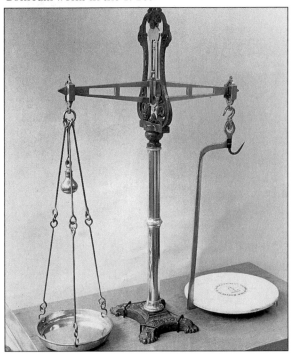

EXPERTS & SPECIALISTS
IN MODERN SHOP FRONTS, INTERIOR FITTINGS,
STRUCTURAL AND
COMPLETE ALTERATIONS.

2018

THE STORES

GROCERIES

TEA EXPERTS

HUDSON BROS

HUDSON BROS

WINES

SPECIALITIES

HUDSON BROS

A typical example of a Parnall high-class ornate shop front and fittings produced at the Coliseum works in the 1920s.

A Parnall 'Superior' Agate counter scale, model 115b of 1895, with a special provision plate hook.

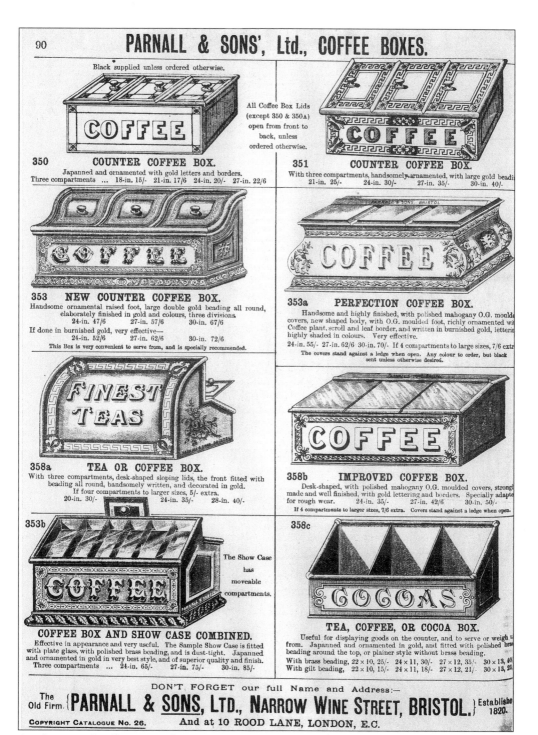

PARNALL & SONS', Ltd., COFFEE BOXES.

Black supplied unless ordered otherwise.

All Coffee Box Lids (except 350 & 350A) open from front to back, unless ordered otherwise.

350   COUNTER COFFEE BOX.
Japanned and ornamented with gold letters and borders.
Three compartments ... 18-in. 15/-   21-in. 17/6   24-in. 20/-   27-in. 22/6

351   COUNTER COFFEE BOX.
With three compartments, handsomely ornamented, with large gold beading.
21-in. 25/-   24-in. 30/-   27-in. 35/-   30-in. 40/-.

353   NEW COUNTER COFFEE BOX.
Handsome ornamental raised foot, large double gold beading all round,
elaborately finished in gold and colours, three divisions.
24-in. 47/6   27-in. 57/6   30-in. 67/6
If done in burnished gold, very effective—
24-in. 52/6   27-in. 62/6   30-in. 72/6
This Box is very convenient to serve from, and is specially recommended.

353a   PERFECTION COFFEE BOX.
Handsome and highly finished, with polished mahogany O.G. moulded
covers, new shaped body, with O.G. moulded foot, richly ornamented with
Coffee plant, scroll and leaf border, and written in burnished gold, lettering
highly shaded in colours. Very effective.
24-in. 55/-   27-in. 62/6   30-in. 70/-   If 4 compartments to large sizes, 7/6 extra.
The covers stand against a ledge when open. Any colour to order, but black
sent unless otherwise desired.

358a   TEA OR COFFEE BOX.
With three compartments, desk-shaped sloping lids, the front fitted with
beading all round, handsomely written, and decorated in gold.
If four compartments to larger sizes, 5/- extra.
20-in. 30/-   24-in. 35/-   28-in. 40/-.

358b   IMPROVED COFFEE BOX.
Desk-shaped, with polished mahogany O.G. moulded covers, strongly
made and well finished, with gold lettering and borders. Specially adapted
for rough wear.   24-in. 35/-   27-in. 42/6   30-in. 50/-.
If 4 compartments to larger sizes, 7/6 extra. Covers stand against a ledge when open.

353b
The Show Case has moveable compartments.

COFFEE BOX AND SHOW CASE COMBINED.
Effective in appearance and very useful. The Sample Show Case is fitted
with plate glass, with polished brass beading, and is dust-tight. Japanned
and ornamented in gold in very best style, and of superior quality and finish.
Three compartments ... 24-in. 65/-   27-in. 75/-   30-in. 85/-.

358c

TEA, COFFEE, OR COCOA BOX.
Useful for displaying goods on the counter, and to serve or weigh
from. Japanned and ornamented in gold, and fitted with polished brass
beading around the top, or plainer style without brass beading.
With brass beading, 22 × 10, 25/-   24 × 11, 30/-   27 × 12, 35/-   30 × 13, 40/-
With gilt beading,   22 × 10, 15/-   24 × 11, 18/-   27 × 12, 21/-   30 × 13, 25/-

A selection of coffee, tea and cocoa counter-type containers advertised in an early Parnall &
Sons catalogue. The company's address was still given as Narrow Wine Street, Bristol.

A Short 827 seaplane after construction by Parnall & Sons Ltd in their Coliseum works, Bristol. Note the radiator above the Sunbeam Nubian engine.

Another view of a Short 827, minus its serial number, completed in the Coliseum works of Parnall & Sons Ltd. Note the drooped ailerons on upper wings.

A Parnall-built Short 827, No. 8255, prepares to alight with its 150hp Sunbeam Nubian throttled back.

One Short Type 184 seaplane (No. 843), like this one seen taxiing, was rebuilt by Parnall's in the Coliseum works during November 1916.

A Parnall-built Short bomber, No. 9771, in Parnall's Coliseum works, with the lower wing and front/rear cockpit coaming for another machine in the foreground.

The 250hp Rolls-Royce Eagle III engine with its neat cowling, installed in Short bomber No. 9771, here in Parnall's Coliseum works, where it is nearing completion in 1916.

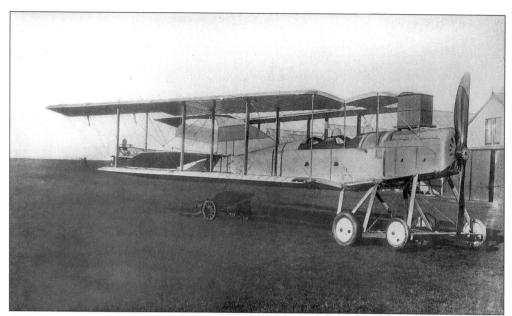

Among the features to note on this Short bomber, identical to a Parnall-built machine, are the folded wings, large radiator atop the engine and cumbersome four-wheel landing gear.

A Parnall-built Hamble Baby seaplane, a single-seat anti-submarine biplane, scout and bomber, powered by a 110/130hp Clerget rotary engine. Note that the bombs are carried beneath the fuselage.

The original Sopwith design incorporating vertical tail surfaces and floats is apparent on the Hamble Baby built by Parnall & Sons. Beneath the serial N.1190 is the Parnall company number (c/n) P.112.

Of 130 Hamble Baby biplanes built by Parnall's, seventy-four emerged as land planes known as Hamble Baby Converts with wide-track landing gear. This one (No. N.2059) has been completed in Parnall & Sons' Coliseum works, Bristol.

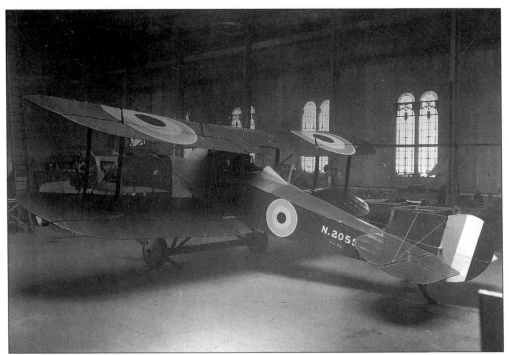

Another view of the Hamble Baby Convert N.2059 in Parnall's Coliseum works. The engine was a 130hp Clerget rotary. Note the Fairey camber gear fitted to the upper wings; this consisted of hinged flaps which operated as ailerons in flight, but when lowered together provided increased lift.

A Parnall-built Avro 504K (E.3254, c/n P.1/6000), powered by a 110hp Le Rhône rotary engine, pictured on Bristol Downs. This was the first of a batch of 130 machines produced for the RAF after it was formed on 1 April 1918.

A group of ladies employed at the Coliseum works of Parnall & Sons Ltd in Park Row, Bristol. The lady sitting in the centre and wearing a hat was probably the forewoman. The wings stacked at the back are for a Parnall-built Avro 504.

A number of Avro 504J trainers were converted to 504K standard by Parnall & Sons Ltd. This 504J (D7103) is a Royal Flying Corps machine in around 1917.

The airframe of an Avro 504K prior to being covered with fabric, having been built under contract in the Coliseum works of Parnall & Sons Ltd. Note the door and windows of the building, which had once been an ice-skating rink. There are many Avro 504 components lying around waiting to become integral parts of other 504 airframes.

At Parnall's Coliseum works, an Avro 504J airframe is converted to 504K configuration by having a 110hp Le Rhône rotary engine installed.

An Avro 504N with a 160/180hp Armstrong Siddeley Lynx engine. This machine (F8713) was originally a Parnall-built 504K converted to 504N standard.

A rare photograph of the one-off Parnall Scout Zepp-chaser (N505). Powered by a 250hp Sunbeam Maori engine, it never flew due to a very low safety factor. It was intended to intercept German Zeppelin airships at night and was thus painted completely black.

Aeronautical Inspection Directorate 3 view plans of Parnall's Scout Zepp-Chaser, taken from a preliminary experimental report, which includes approximate dimensions. A .303in Lewis gun was mounted on the starboard side of the fuselage at an angle of forty-five degrees.

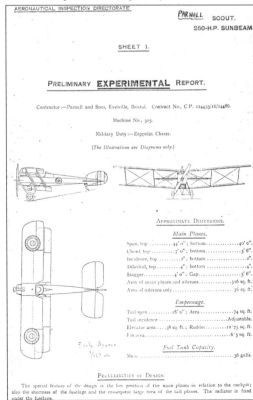

Parnall's second aircraft design was the Panther two-seat carrier-borne Fleet Spotter reconnaissance biplane with a 230hp Bentley BR 2 rotary engine. The prototype (N.91) shown here has the pilot's forward-firing Vickers machine-gun fitted, but this was later removed from this and all Panthers. The landing gear was later improved, a hydrovane was fitted to prevent nosing over in the event of a 'ditching' and inflatable flotation bags were installed.

The fuselage of a Parnall Panther under construction at the Coliseum works. Note the belt-driven machinery just visible on the other side of the dividing partition.

Parnall Panther (N.96) with its Isle of Grain-type flotation bags inflated. Notice the hydrovane fitted ahead of the landing gear to prevent nosing over.

To facilitate stowage on aircraft carriers, Parnall's Panther featured a folding fuselage. Tail unit control cables were housed in a channel on the starboard side of the fuselage to avoid chafing.

A hand-swinging start-up for the 230hp Bentley BR 2 aboard a Royal Navy aircraft carrier, probably HMS *Argus*, *c.* 1921.

Two
Fishponds, The War and Beyond

Following the vacation in 1919 of the Fishponds site by aero-engine manufacturer Cosmos (they took it over in 1918 from the original owners, Brazil Straker), Parnall & Sons Ltd acquired it in 1923. Until the 1930s they had manufactured high-class shopfittings, but prior to, during and after the Second World War, they produced numerous components for several types of aircraft. The main layout of the Fishponds site is well portrayed in this 1960s aerial view of the factory.

The first aero-engine contract at Fishponds (Brazil Straker) was for the overhaul of Curtiss OX-5 engines used in Royal Naval Air Service (RNAS) Curtiss JN-4 'Jenny' trainers, like this one seen at RNAS Redcar.

Under Brazil Straker, Fishponds turned out 2,500 Rolls-Royce engines during the First World War including the 75hp Hawk. Among the types of aircraft powered by Hawks was this RNAS submarine scout airship, SS Z19.

Another Fishponds-built engine was the Rolls-Royce Falcon. An RAF Blackburn Kangaroo, B.0076 of No 246 Squadron, runs up its two 255hp Falcons at Seaton Carew, from where it flew anti-U-boat operations.

A 190hp Rolls-Royce Falcon, built at Fishponds, powered this Bristol F2A fighter, A.3343, of the Royal Flying Corps (RFC). The later F2B fighter had an uprated 275hp Falcon III engine.

The Fairey F.2 three-seat long-range naval fighter and general purpose biplane (here, No. 3704) was first flown in 1917. Seen here with wings folded, it was powered by a pair of Rolls-Royce Falcons built at Fishponds.

This ex-RAF Martinsyde F.4 fighter, 'civilianized' as K152 and powered by a 275hp Rolls-Royce Falcon III built at Fishponds, is at Hendon on Aerial Derby day, 21 June 1919. It came in second at an average speed of 124.61mph.

A number of French-designed static V-8 air-cooled 80hp Renault engines were also produced at Brazil Straker's Fishponds works. This Avro 548 (G-EBFM) is powered by one of these engines.

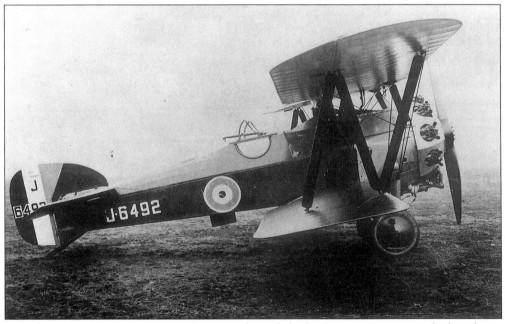

Bristol Badger II, J6492, was used as a Fishponds-built Cosmos Jupiter test-bed and was experimentally fitted with a variety of engine cowlings.

A Bristol Bullet, G-EATS, of 1919 designed as a test-bed to study the effects of high speed manoeuvres on the Cosmos Jupiter engine. Its top speed was 155mph.

Designed by Roy Fedden (later Sir Roy), this was the famous Jupiter engine, created at Fishponds as the Cosmos Jupiter and later to earn added fame under the Bristol banner, when it powered a number of well known military and civilian aircraft.

Initially fitted with Armstrong Siddeley Jaguar engines, this giant tri-motored Handley Page 9a Hampstead airliner (G-EBLE) later flew with Imperial Airways, powered by three Bristol Jupiter IVs.

Powered by a Bristol Jupiter engine, this Gloster Gamecock fighter (J7910) was used on anti-flutter tests with narrow-chord ailerons.

A 'golden age' indeed: a Short S.17 Kent flying-boat G-ABFC *Satyrus* flies gracefully over a calm sea driven by her four 555hp Bristol Jupiter XFBM air-cooled radial engines.

As British as they come! A Bristol Bulldog II fighter (K1085) which flew with 17 and later 29 Squadrons of the RAF, powered by a 490hp Bristol Jupiter VIIF.

Towards the end of the 1930s, Parnall's at Fishponds were producing airframes and components for DH Tiger Moth trainers. This example is N9469/'B' in 1942 which served with No. 9 EFTS.

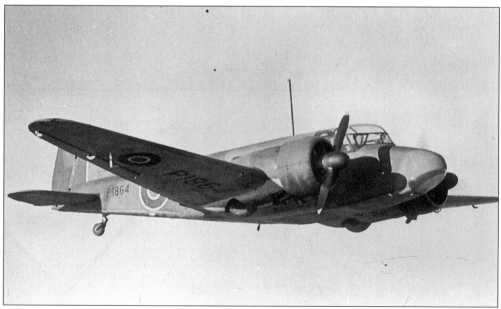

A large number of wings for Airspeed Oxford twin-engine trainers were produced by Parnall's at Lodge Causeway. This Oxford (P1864) is seen in RAF service during the mid-1940s.

An ungainly bird, Fairey's Barracuda nevertheless gave yeoman service as a torpedo and dive-bomber in the Fleet Air Arm. Parnall's at Fishponds produced the wing flaps for Barracudas.

The first RAF four-engined bomber was the Short Stirling, for which Parnall's built complete fins at Fishponds. This machine being 'bombed up' is with No. 7 Squadron.

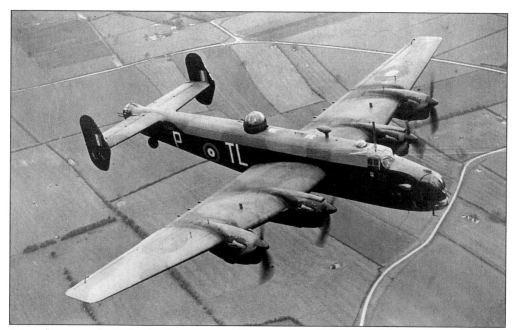

Wing flaps were built for the four-engined Handley Page Halifax RAF bomber by Parnall's at Fishponds. This Halifax II (W7676/'TL-P') is seen in service with 35 Squadron of RAF Bomber Command.

Parnall's also produced tailplanes for the Bristol Beaufighter twin-engined fighter. This is a Mk I, T4638/'NG-F' of 604 Squadron, in night finish.

Numerous components were built at Fishponds by Parnall's for the DH Mosquito. Seen here is DZ313, a Mk IV from the fourth production batch.

Many fuselages for Airspeed Horsa troop-carrying gliders were produced by Parnall's at Fishponds. Used in Normandy and the landings at Arnhem, these could convey vehicles and troops as shown here in an exercise in 1949.

In 1952 Parnall's built DH Venom jet-fighter fuselages at Fishponds. These Venom FB1s are with 98 Squadron RAF in Germany during the 1950s.

Tailplanes for the four-engined DH Heron also came from Parnall's at Fishponds. This Heron is in service with the Royal Jordanian Air Force.

Lodge Causeway works produced interior components for the Bristol 170 freighter. This machine (9696) is seen serving with the Royal Canadian Air Force.

Parnall's Fishponds factory supplied wings, fins, rudders and ailerons for the Bristol Britannia turboprop airliner. This is Britannia 311 G-AOVA on a test flight in Bristol Aeroplane colours.

During 1955 interior fittings were produced at the Fishponds works by Parnall's for the DH 106 Comet airliner. Here Comet LV-PLM is in the colours of Aerolíneas Argentinas.

The 1960s saw Parnall's at Fishponds manufacturing metal components for the Hawker Siddeley (HS) 125 executive jet. This view shows a HS 125-800 in Australian service as VH-HSP in around 1985.

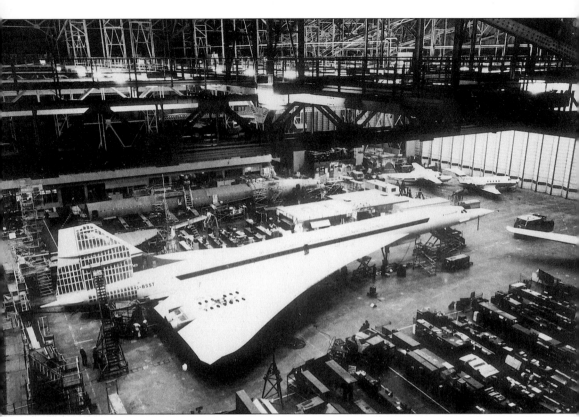

Furniture items for Concorde, the world's first supersonic airliner, came from the Parnall & Sons Fishponds works in the 1960s. Here Concorde 002 (G-BSST) undergoes final assembly at British Aircraft Corporation (as it was then) at Filton.

A BAC/SUD Concorde in service. Here G-BOAE of British Airways is on finals into London Heathrow.

Three
George Parnall & Co.
1920-1935

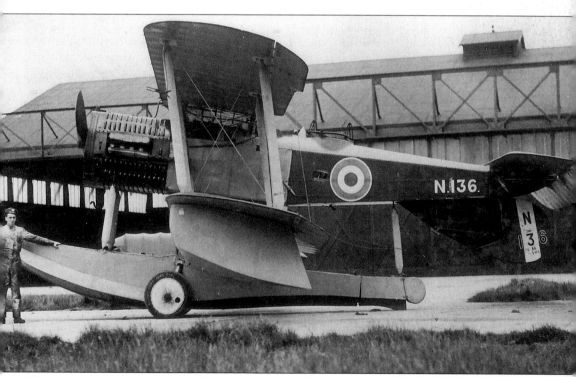

The first Parnall's Puffin (N.136), powered by a 450hp Napier Lion II water-cooled engine. Here the main central float has been redesigned to have an upward curve to its bow. Note the unusual tail design.

Because W.T. Avery, the controlling body of Parnall & Sons Ltd in Bristol, could not agree with George Parnall's desire to expand the firm's aviation interests after the First World War, he resigned as head of the firm in 1919 and inaugurated his own company at the Coliseum works, Park Row, Bristol, as George Parnall & Co., later moving to Yate. George Parnall introduced a number of innovative ideas which were applied practically in the fields of shopfitting and aeroplane manufacture. In this personally signed photograph, George Parnall stands in front of the prototype Parnall Elf biplane at Yate in 1929.

Displayed at the 1920 Hendon Air Show is George Parnall & Co.'s second Puffin, N.137. Note that the main central float has been further modified.

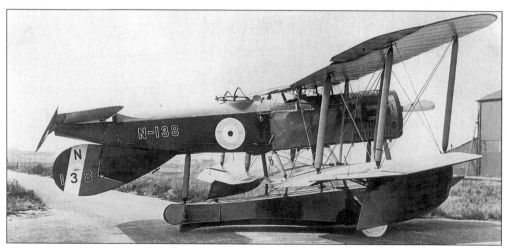

The third and final Parnall Puffin (N.138), fitted with a water rudder at the tail of the main float. Note the method of applying rudder serial number, the large wing-tip floats and the gun ring in the rear cockpit.

George Parnall, with his back to the camera and wearing the overcoat and scarf, is watching the first flight preparations at Filton for the single-seat Parnall Plover naval fighter, N.160.

The third prototype Parnall Plover (N162), powered by a 385hp Armstrong Siddeley Jaguar engine. The designation number 9 on the fuselage indicates the Plover's exhibition number in the New Types Park at the RAF Hendon Air Show in 1923.

PARNALL PLOVER AMPHIBIAN
BRISTOL JUPITER ENGINE

Powered by a 436hp Bristol Jupiter, Parnall Plover N9610, seen here at Yate, was the only production machine built as a twin-float amphibian.

The first of ten production Parnall Plovers, N9608, is pictured at Filton, with a 436hp Bristol Jupiter IV engine. In the cockpit is Captain Norman MacMillan, a freelance test pilot who later became chief test pilot to Fairey Aviation. The ten Parnall Plovers produced served with the Fleet Air Arm in Fighter Flight Nos 403 and 404.

A civilian Plover, G-EBON (ex-N9705). Entered in the 1926 King's Cup Air Race, it retired from the event with fuel feed problems. G-EBON crashed and was written off in January 1929.

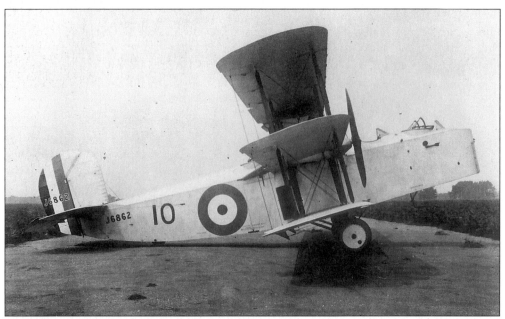

Wearing its exhibition number 10 for the 1923 RAF Hendon Air Pageant is Parnall Possum J6862, a large triplane with one 450hp Napier Lion engine driving two propellers via gears and extension shafts.

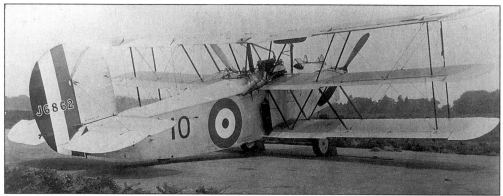

A Parnall's Possum triplane, showing the unorthodox method of mounting a 450hp Napier Lion engine in the upper fuselage to drive two outboard propellers. J6862 was the first of two built.

This view shows to advantage the Possum's size and triplane layout.

The second Parnall Possum, J6863, at the A&AEE, Martlesham Heath, c. 1925. Notice the hinged radiator swung out on the starboard side of the fuselage.

The Parnall Pixie in original form as built for the 1923 'Motor Glider' or light aeroplane trials, at Lympne. The engine is a $3\frac{1}{2}$ hp (500cc) two-cylinder Douglas. Here the Pixie is in Mk I configuration with large wings fitted for the fuel consumption tests.

An early type of fin and rudder are apparent on this Parnall Pixie II, so designated through its more powerful 6hp (736cc) Douglas and 18ft wing span.

In biplane form, the Pixie IIIA was powered by a 35hp Blackburne Thrush engine. Here it is entered as No. 19 in the 1924 Light Aeroplane Trials. In the background is the Pixie III monoplane, No. 18.

During 1926 both Parnall Pixie IIIs were converted to permanent monoplanes, with 32hp Bristol Cherub III engines. This close-up shows mounting details of the Cherub engine in a Pixie III.

This Pixie III, G-EBJG, took part in the Light Aeroplane Trials as No. 14 in September 1926. It was piloted by Frank Courtney and came in fourth in the week-long event.

George Geach Parnall at his Yate desk in 1930. The pile of books at the far left are *RAF Quarterly* magazines for 1930 with the year's *Air Estimates* on top.

Part of the accounts office at George Parnall's Yate factory in 1930. On the wall hangs a Wright's 1930 timetable with several advertisements on the cover.

The woodworking shop at George Parnall & Co. in Yate in 1930.

Part of the shopfitting and cabinet shop at George Parnall & Co., 1930. The electric lighting, workbenches and various tools are worthy of note.

A fine head-on view of the Parnall Perch two-seat naval training biplane at the MAEE, Felixstowe, in April 1927, where it was flown by Frank Courtney.

A close-up of the 270hp Rolls-Royce Falcon III 12-cylinder Vee water-cooled engine, uncowled and mounted in the one-off Parnall Perch, N217.

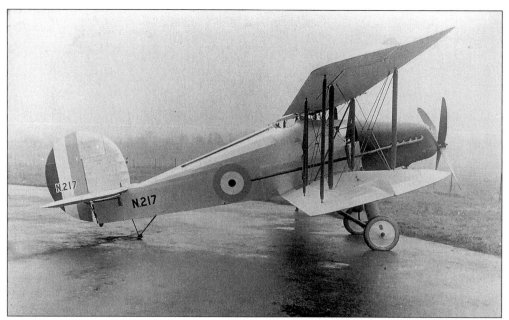

The Parnall Perch naval trainer in land plane form at the A&AEE, Martlesham Heath, in early April 1927.

Parnall's Perch (N217) in twin-float seaplane configuration, on its dolly and trestled at the rear at the MAEE at Felixstowe in April 1927.

A Parnall Peto (N181) at Yate in 1926. Designed to operate from an 'M' class submarine, it is here powered by a 135hp Armstrong Siddeley Mongoose engine and has duralumin floats with water rudders.

After being rebuilt as N255, the original Peto (N181) is on the hoist of its mother ship, the ill-fated submarine M2, which sank off Portland with all hands and the Peto on 26 January 1932.

Parnall Peto N181 at Felixstowe in 1925, with a pair of Saunders 'Consuta' floats and a 127.8hp Bristol Lucifer IV engine.

The second Parnall Peto (N182) at Yate in 1926. It has a 135hp Bristol Lucifer engine, enlarged fin and rudder, and duralumin floats.

A rear view of Parnall Pike N202, a two- or three-seater naval reconnaissance biplane. The distance between the rear observer/gunner's cockpit and the pilot is apparent in this shot.

The Parnall Pike N202, powered by a 450hp Napier Lion engine, at Yate aerodrome prior to a test flight in March 1927. Note the Warren girder interplane struts which removed the need for bracing wires.

Parnall Pike N202 prepares for another test flight at Yate in 1927. Standing in front of the port wing (outboard) is test pilot Frank Courtney.

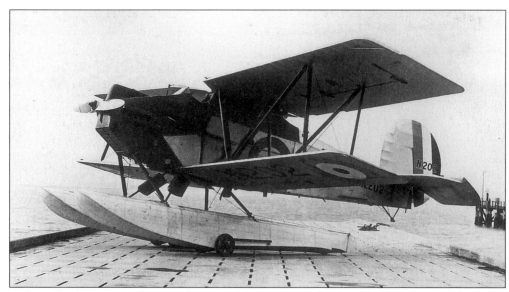

A Parnall Pike in twin-float seaplane configuration at Felixstowe for its MAEE trials during 1927.

A copy of an original drawing by George Parnall & Co. of the Parnall Imp two-seater sporting biplane with an Armstrong Siddeley Genet engine.

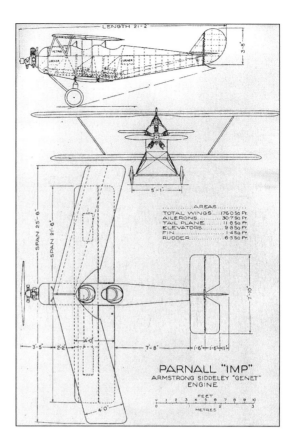

The Parnall Imp two-seater and its 80hp Armstrong Siddeley Genet II engine, registered G-EBTE. Note the single interplane strut and upper wing sweep-back.

The Parnall Imp sporting biplane G-EBTE outside a hangar at Yate in 1928. Notice the practice of applying the letter 'G' to all tail surfaces.

In updated form with a cowled 65hp Pobjoy 'P' radial engine and headrest fairing, Parnall's Imp carries the racing number 18.

A prototype Parnall Pipit single-seat naval fighter under construction at George Parnall & Co., Yate, c. 1927-28. It was powered by a 495hp Rolls-Royce F.XI 12-cylinder Vee liquid-cooled engine.

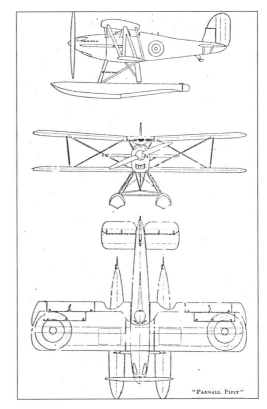

"PARNALL PIPIT"

A copy taken from an original Parnall drawing of the Pipit naval fighter in its proposed twin-float seaplane configuration.

The first prototype Parnall Pipit (N232) receiving final adjustments outside Yate works prior to its initial test flight, piloted by Flt Lt J. 'Oojie' Noakes.

Despite its aesthetic lines, Parnall's Pipit was a victim of flutter. Note the gun trough in the side of the fuselage and the cumbersome tail skid.

Wreckage of Parnall's Pipit naval fighter (N232) after violent tail flutter had snapped the sternpost causing the fin and rudder to break away. Test pilot Flt Lt H.N. 'Poppy' Pope parachuted to safety, but the loss of this second Pipit dashed George Parnall's hopes of a lucrative production order for this aesthetically pleasing biplane. Unusually both Parnall Pipits were allotted the same serial number, N232.

A copy of the 1929 cover of the George Parnall & Co. brochure, advertising their Parasol experimental and research monoplane of which two were built.

GEORGE PARNALL & Co.

[Photo]   [R.A.F. Official Crown Copyright Reserved]

Parnall Parasol Monoplane

Designed to fulfil the function of securing true full-scale data, and of measuring the aerodynamic forces acting on the wings of an aircraft. See page 326 of this Annual.

Full particulars on application to:

GEORGE PARNALL & Co.
COLISEUM WORKS, PARK ROW, BRISTOL

Phone: Bristol 4773 (3 lines)   Telegrams: "Warplanes, Bristol"

Phone: YATE AERODROME,
"Chipping" Sodbury, 50   GLOS.   Telegrams:
                                         "Warplanes, Yate"

Parnall Parasol (K1288) with a camera mounted above its rear fuselage to record the behaviour of wool tufts, clearly seen here attached to the upper surfaces of an experimental wing.

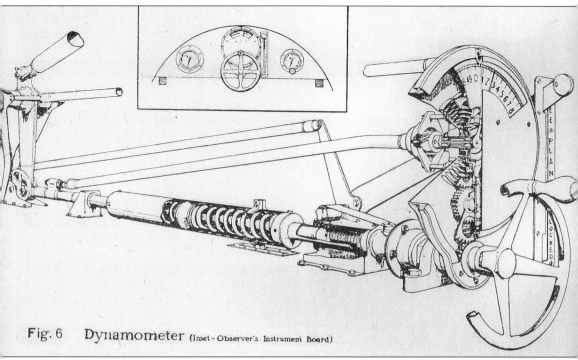

Fig. 6   Dynamometer (Inset - Observer's Instrument Board)

A 1926 diagram showing the dynamometer gear system and mechanism, with observer's control wheel and (inset) instrument panel, incorporated into the Parnall Parasol monoplane. By this means accurate measurements could be taken of forces acting on an experimental wing at various angles of incidence created by a special swinging frame.

The Parasol experimental monoplane revealed the research and versatile capabilities of George Parnall & Co., as exemplified here with the Plover, Pixie and Possum triplane lined up for comparison.

A Parnall Parasol (K1288), powered by a 226hp supercharged Armstrong Siddeley Lynx IV engine. Here a parallel-chord, fully slotted wing of RAF 28 Section is fitted. Note the recorder lowered below the port wing.

Parnall Parasol K1228 at Yate, built to research forces acting on wings at various angles of incidence. Special apparatus allowed the wing some restricted freedom of movement in relation to the fuselage.

Three wing incidence positions could be obtained with this high tensile steel tube swinging frame. It was part of the Parnall Parasol research monoplane of which two were built at Yate. Supported on this 'cradle', the wing also had high tensile steel bracing struts.

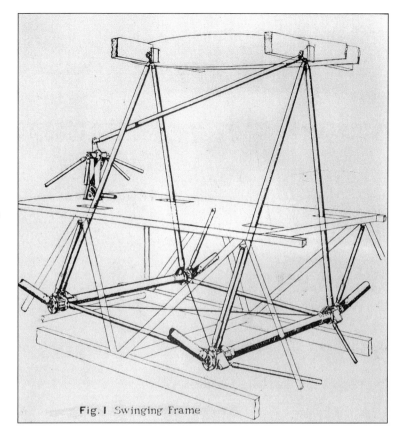

Fig. I Swinging Frame

Parnall Parasol K1228 at Yate. Provision to alter wing incidence is clearly visible in the fuselage slots at the base of the wing bracing struts.

A view of the planning office at George Parnall's Yate works. The date is Friday 28 November 1930.

A general view of the cabinet-making shop at George Parnall & Co., Yate, 1930. This side of the business was sold to Avery's at Fishponds in 1932 after they faced strong competition from George Parnall & Co.

GEORGE PARNALL & Co.

INTERNATIONAL AERO EXHIBITION

STAND 92

Phone: RIVERSIDE 5569.

PARNALL ELF

The New Two-Seater Light Plane

with

105 h.p. HERMES ENGINE

as

:: Land Machine or Seaplane ::

Full Particulars on application to:

GEORGE PARNALL & CO.

COLISEUM WORKS, PARK ROW, BRISTOL.

Telephone: BRISTOL 4773 (3 lines).   Telegrams: "WARPLANES, BRISTOL".

At the 1929 International Aero Exhibition held at London's Olympia, George Parnall & Co. featured their Elf two-seat sporting biplane on Stand 92 as shown on this contemporary advertisement by the company. The address still refers to both the Coliseum works at Bristol and Yate aerodrome.

Powered by a 105hp ADC Cirrus Hermes 1, the Parnall Elf prototype two-seater is seen here at Yate with its biplane wings folded to facilitate transportation through gateways, or stowage where space was at a premium.

A country setting for prototype Parnall Elf after receiving its civil registration G-AAFH. It was sold to Lord Apsley of Badminton in December 1932. Notice the full-span ailerons on this machine.

HRH the Duke of York (later HM King George VI) has the Parnall Elf explained to him by George Parnall at stand 92 in the 1929 International Aero Exhibition, Olympia, London. They are standing by the Elf's tail with the Parnall Peto submarine-borne machine on the right, its starboard float and struts just visible.

Another view of Parnall Elf G-AAFH in its rural setting. The Warren girder-type interplane struts and neatly cowled engine are noteworthy.

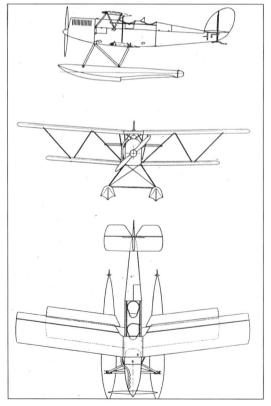

A three-view drawing taken from a 1929 George Parnall & Co. brochure showing the Parnall Elf in twin-float seaplane configuration. There is no record of the Elf having flown as a floatplane.

The as yet unregistered Parnall Elf prototype in full cry over Yate aerodrome in 1929, with a highly polished cowling enclosing its ADC Cirrus Hermes.

A rear view of the prototype Parnall Elf with its wings folded to provide a very narrow width of only 7ft 1in, an asset for ground handling.

Folding wings give Parnall's Elf a naval touch, but the purpose was to induce potential buyers to see the advantage of a machine that could easily be pushed on the ground and required little space.

The only surviving Parnall Elf out of three built at Yate (G-AAFH/IO/IN), G-AAIN. Built in 1932, it had a 120hp Cirrus Hermes II engine. Acquired by Lord Apsley, stored throughout the Second World War and later purchased by the Shuttleworth Trust, Elf G-AAIN was fully restored and on 25 June 1980 made its first flight for over forty years. G-AAIN is seen here at Old Warden in June 1981.

In 1930 George Parnall & Co. built a small single-seat flying-boat, the Prawn (S.1576), to determine the effects of prow-mounted engines in flying-boats. A 65hp Ricardo-Burt engine, mounted above the bow, was pivoted at the rear to enable the thrust angle to be altered by raising the complete power unit to a maximum twenty-two degrees. A very small diameter four-bladed propeller also reduced spray effects, its spinner forming the prow of this unique, tiny flying-boat.

In this view the Parnall Prawn (S1576) has its engine in the raised position and shows to advantage the small diameter four-bladed propeller and general layout.

Used at the MAEE, Felixstowe, on experimental and research duties, Parnall's Prawn (S.1576) is seen here with its engine in the raised position.

This time with its engine lowered, the Prawn is pictured at Yate aerodrome in 1930. Notice the radiator perched atop the bow/engine line.

Harold Bolas, chief aircraft designer to Parnall & Sons and George Parnall & Co. from 1917 until 1929, in front of Elf G-AAFH. This was Bolas's last design for Parnall's before leaving for America in 1929. There he joined fellow countryman Captain R.J. Goodman Crouch OBE to form the Crouch-Bolas Aircraft Co. In the mid-1930s they produced the Dragonfly, a promising STOL biplane, but financial problems forced Crouch-Bolas to close in 1937.

The Crouch-Bolas Dragonfly STOL biplane of 1934 designed by Harold Bolas, powered by two 125hp Menasco engines. Its US registration is X13262.

Another angle on the Harold Bolas-designed Crouch-Bolas 'Dragonfly'. Note the twin fins and rudders.

H.V. Clarke replaced Harold Bolas at George Parnall & Co., designing the G.4/31 general purpose biplane K2772, seen here making a low pass over Yate, flown by test pilot Captain Howard Saint.

Powered by a 690hp Bristol Pegasus IM3 radial, the Parnall G.4/31 was the last aircraft designed and built by George Parnall & Co. It is seen here at the A&AEE, Martlesham, for trials in 1935.

A revealing picture of the Parnall G.4/31 general purpose biplane prior to its airframe being fabric-covered. Note the unusual shape of the tail unit.

From this angle Parnall's G.4/31 has a certain aesthetic quality, with its upper gull wing, ring cowling surrounding the Pegasus engine and streamlined wheel spats.

Four
Sub-Contracts

The Cierva Autogiro Co., formed in Britain during 1926, assigned most of its production contracts to Avro, but George Parnall & Co. produced two under sub-contract, the C.10 (military) and C.11 (civilian) machines. Here the C.10 (J9038) nears completion at Yate in 1927, revealing its 82hp Armstrong Siddeley Genet engine and mountings, the stub wings and horn-balanced elevators. A Parnall Imp (G-EBTE) is in the background.

Rotor support structure, landing gear layout and engine mountings are clearly visible here on the Parnall-built Cierva C.10 autogiro J9038.

Standing at Yate aerodrome in early April 1928, the Cierva C.10 (Parnall-built) military autogiro J9038. Note the large paddle-shaped rotor blades.

A rear view of Parnall/Cierva C.10 autogiro J9038. Note the rotor support system and stub wings. The Parnall part numbers on the fin and rudder are P1/5084/T.S.4 and P1/5081/T.S.1 respectively.

On 26 April 1926, the Parnall/Cierva C.10 (J9038) came to grief during its taxiing tests at Yate aerodrome.

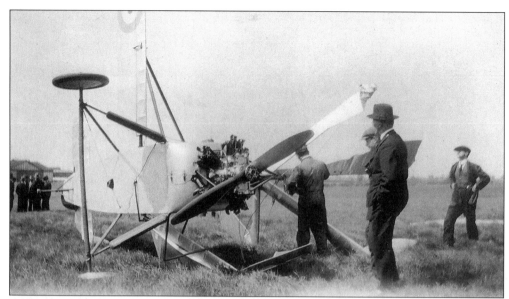

In this frontal view of the damaged C.10 autogiro taken a little later, George Parnall (nearest the camera) surveys the overturned machine.

The Parnall-built Civil C.11 autogiro (G-EBQG) with a 120hp ADC Airdisco engine. It crashed at Yate and, after repairs, ended its days with Air Service Training, Hamble, as an instructional airframe.

The drawing office at George Parnall & Co., Yate, 1930. Note the electric lighting system, roller blinds on the windows and 'T' squares hanging on the wall to the right.

Shop counters and cabinets under construction in the shopfitting section of George Parnall & Co. at Yate in 1930. The men's aprons and foreman's white smock are typical of that period in industry.

At least thirty de Havilland DH 9A biplanes were rebuilt, or built as new, for the RAF by George Parnall & Co. at Yate under Air Ministry contracts. These provided the firm with its 'bread and butter' work in the 1920s. DH 9As were powered by a 400hp American Liberty 12 engine, and became a regular RAF workhorse in the 1920s and early 1930s. Here is a line-up of DH 9As of 'A' Flight, 4 Flying Training School, Abu Sueir, Egypt.

Parnall's built twelve dual-control DH 9A trainers for the RAF (J8483-J8494) similar to this machine (E8742) flying over Karachi in 1924.

This DH 9A (H3631), akin to those built/rebuilt by Parnall's, is at a snow-covered aerodrome in 1930. It has special underwing store carriers fitted and was built by Vulcan Motor Engineering.

The Hendy 302 of 1929 (G-AAVT), with tandem two-seat enclosed cockpit and powered by a 105hp Cirrus Hermes I engine, was a civil contract for George Parnall. It is seen here over Yate in 1930.

Considerable updating in 1933-34 by C.S. Napier resulted in the Hendy 302 being re-designated the Hendy 302A. With a 130hp Cirrus Hermes IV engine, it appeared as shown here in 1934.

The Hendy 302A as an entrant in the 1934 King's Cup Race, wearing racing number 19. Originally built as the Hendy 302 by George Parnall & Co. and owned by Captain E.W. Percival, it went to Cirrus Hermes Engineering as a flying test-bed. Sold to Carill S. Napier, it was updated to have a 130hp Cirrus Hermes IV, some structural improvements, fully glazed cockpit and streamlined wheel spats. Still with its original Hendy 302 registration, G-AAVT, the 302A averaged 133.5mph in the 1934 King's Cup Race.

After his Hendy 302, Basil 'Hendy' Henderson designed this two-seat Heck (G-ACTC), built by Westland in 1934. Its retractable landing gear proved troublesome and, when a production run of six Heck 2Cs was made by Parnall Aircraft Ltd, they had fixed undercarriages and were built as three-seaters.

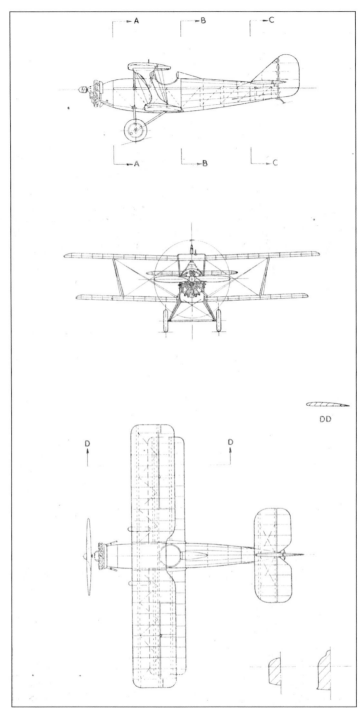

First flown in August 1932, the diminutive Miles Satyr sporting biplane was built for F.G. Miles by George Parnall & Co at Yate. Power was provided by a 75hp Pobjoy 'R' radial engine. Its top speed was 125mph and it could climb to 1,400ft in one minute. This three-view drawing (ex-T.I. Jackson archives) shows the Satyr to have a half-size contemporary single-seat fighter look. It was extremely aerobatic.

Mr F.G. Miles in the cockpit of his Parnall-built Satyr biplane, running up the Pobjoy 'R' engine, at Yate in 1932. Its wingspan was only 21ft and length 17ft 8in.

At rest on a wet aerodrome, a Miles Satyr (G-ABVG) built by George Parnall & Co., shows the single 'I' interplane struts, and comparatively large wheels and propeller.

The first female employee of George Parnall & Co. was Miss May (later Mrs Margaret Fry), who joined the company late in 1925. In this 1938 photograph Mrs Fry (arrowed) is forewoman. From left to right, standing: Miss Lancaster, Mrs Heard, Miss Merrett, Mrs Fry, Miss Barton, Miss Davis, Miss Tanner, Miss Gowen. Sitting: Miss Wilkins, Miss Wilcox, Miss Matthews, Miss Bezer. By then the company had been sold to Nash & Thompson Ltd (of Frazer-Nash).

The machine shop at George Parnall & Co., Yate, in 1930. This typical working environment of the day (poor lighting and belt-driven machinery) would give a safety officer of today a shock!

The metal-fitting shop at George Parnall & Co., Yate, in 1930. Here metal components were shaped to the requirements of other departments.

Although George Parnall & Co. built the first production batch of Percival Gull Four monoplanes, the prototype (G-ABUR) seen here was designed and built in 1932 at Maidstone, Kent, by Capt. Edgar Percival and his team. Powered by a 130hp Cirrus Hermes IV engine, it flew in the 1932 King's Cup Race, covering the course at an average of 142.73mph.

The prototype Gull Four with revised canopy and new paint scheme. It has race number 40 on its fin and rudder.

A Parnall-built Percival Gull Four, G-ABUV, with a 130hp Cirrus Hermes IV engine. It crashed at Nice, France, on 2 November 1936 when owned by M. Maxwell.

A Parnall-built Percival Gull Four (G-ACPA/'30') powered by a 160hp Napier Javelin III four-cylinder inverted inline air-cooled engine.

Some Parnall-built Gull Fours were converted to Gull Six standard (with a 200hp DH Gipsy Six engine) like this Gull Six RAF AX866 (ex-G-ADPR), c. 1942.

Five
Parnall Aircraft Ltd, 1935-1946

The first of six production Parnall Heck 2C cabin monoplanes, G-AEGH, standing on Yate aerodrome in the autumn of 1936.

A group of Parnall employees with a Heck 2C at Yate. At the extreme left is test pilot Crosby Warren who was over 6ft 8in tall. He was killed later testing a Gloster Meteor jet fighter.

Heck 2C K8853 went to the A&AEE, Martlesham, on 1 April 1937. Transferring to the RAE later, it was initially employed on Browning machine-gun installation trials.

With its 200hp DH Gipsy Six engine and three-seat accommodation, Parnall's Heck 2C made a suitable communications aircraft during the Second World War. It is seen here in wartime camouflage.

As No. 33, Parnall Heck 2C (G-AEGI) is ready for the 1950 King's Cup Race, in which it made seventh place. After the race it collided with a civilian Spitfire (G-AISU) and was badly damaged.

Something of a Miles Magister look-alike, this was Parnall's last design, the T.1/37 Type 382, known as the Parnall Heck Mk III. Power was provided by a 200hp DH Gipsy VI engine.

Carrying class 'B' marking JI, the Parnall Type 382 at the A&AEE, Martlesham, for trials with its camber-changing flaps lowered.

With its 200hp DH Gipsy Six engine in full cry, the Parnall Type 382 (Spec. T.1/37) climbs away from Yate wearing class 'B' marking JI.

Camber-changing flaps, elevator trim tabs, tandem cockpits and swivelling tail wheel are clearly seen in this view of Parnall's Type 382 trainer.

A murky backdrop at the A&AEE, Martlesham, for the Parnall Type 382 two-seat primary trainer. In this head-on view the clean lines of what was control-wise an innovative basic trainer are apparent.

No production order was made for Parnall's Type 382 trainer. It became G-AFKF, was impressed into RAF service as R9138 with 24 Squadron, ending its days as instructional airframe 3600M.

To counteract slipstream problems with the rear gun position on Hawker Demon two-seat fighters, Frazer-Nash/Parnall's produced a hydraulically-operated open turret nicknamed 'lobster-back' due to its segmented back shield. A number were built and fitted to Demons at Yate by Parnall's as shown here; the type became known as Turret Demons.

Later delivered to No. 23 Squadron, this standard Hawker Demon (K2842) has the original Demon rear cockpit layout and gun mounting.

The crest of No. 64 Squadron is on the fin of this Turret Demon (K4496), which has the 'lobster-back' Frazer-Nash segmented turret installed. Compare this with the standard Demon above.

Gun positions on early Vickers
Wellington bombers were updated to
include the power-operated Frazer-
Nash nose turret built at Parnall's
and shown here.

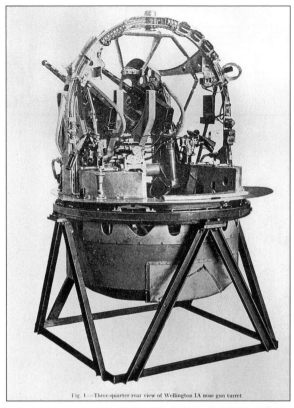

Fig. 1—Three-quarter rear view of Wellington IA nose gun turret

Powered by two 1,050hp Bristol Pegasus engines, this Vickers Wellington Ic (P9249) is
equipped with Parnall-built Frazer-Nash nose and tail turrets.

Parnall-built Frazer-Nash nose and tail turrets were fitted to Armstrong Whitworth's Whitley bomber. This was N1380/DY-R of 102 Squadron.

In matt black finish, this Whitley (Z6640) was with 78 Squadron, but is seen here as Y-Yoke of 1484 Flight. The Parnall-built Frazer-Nash tail turret can be clearly seen.

The crew of a RAF Bomber Command Whitley IV about to board their 102 Squadron machine in 1940 Note the Parnall-built turret and covered over gun muzzle.

The tailplane for the prototype Armstrong Whitworth Ensign four-engined airliner was built by Parnall Aircraft Ltd. Registered G-ADSR, it was the flagship of Imperial Airways' fleet.

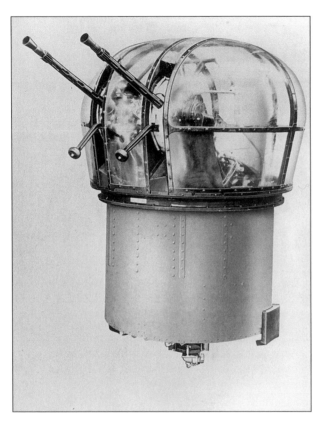

Armed with twin .303in Browning machine-guns, the power-operated Parnall FN 150 turret was fitted in a dorsal (mid-upper) position on Avro Lancaster and Short Stirling III heavy bombers of the RAF.

A Short Stirling III (BF509) of RAF Bomber Command early in 1943. The Parnall-built VN 150 turret is clearly seen atop the fuselage.

The Frazer-Nash nose, dorsal and tail turrets built by Parnall's at Yate are well defined on the Avro Lancaster, R5689/VN-N, of 50 Squadron RAF in 1943.

Short Sunderland flying-boats were also armed with Parnall-built FN turrets. This machine, coded RB-A, is serving here with UK-based 10 Squadron, Royal Australian Air Force.

The strange-looking dorsal turret on this Blackburn Botha was an FN 7 built by Parnall's at Yate. The Botha, intended as a torpedo-bomber, ended up as a trainer. This machine is L6507/IM.

Modified FN 7 dorsal turret was fitted to Avro's Manchester, plus FN 5 nose and FN 4A or FN 20 tail turrets, all built at Yate by Parnall's. This aircraft was L7515/EM-S (S-Sugar) of 201 Squadron.

An aerial photograph of Yate taken on 22 August 1939 by a German reconnaissance aircraft through light cloud. In the resulting negative both Parnall's and Newman's works (the latter produced artillery shells) were outlined. The importance of Parnall's works in relation to bomber gun turret production was documented and strongly emphasized to Luftwaffe pilots and crews.

111

Flugzeugzellenfabrik Parnall Aircraft Co. Ltd., Yate (74 51)

Das Werk ist Haupthersteller von „Doppel- und Vierling-MG-Türmen", die u. a. als Heckstände in englische Kampfflugzeuge eingebaut werden. Parnall ist außer der Firma Nash & Thompson, London-Tolworth (78 15, lfd. Nr. 63), der einzige Hersteller dieser Türme, jedoch von wesentlich größerer Leistungsfähigkeit.

Eine Zerstörung des Werkes würde die Kampfflugzeugausbringung stark beeinträchtigen.

Das Werk liegt an der Bahnlinie Bristol—Wickwar, etwa 2 km nördlich der Doppelkreuzung von Westerleigh. An dem Werk zweigt eine Bahnlinie im Bogen nach NW (Thornbury) ab. Unmittelbar am Werk liegt der Flugplatz Yate (10 284).

A German directive showing the enemy's concern at Parnall's output, and how destruction of the Yate site would disrupt production of RAF bombers.

PARNALL AIRCRAFT FACTORY YATE (7451)

THIS FACTORY IS THE MAIN PRODUCER OF "2 x 4MG TURRETS" WHICH ARE FITTED IN ENGLISH FIGHTER PLANES.

PARNALL IS A SUBSIDIARY OF NASH & THOMPSON LONDON & TOLWORTH (78 15 REF NR. 63) & IS THE ONLY PRODUCER OF THESE TURRETS & ARE ABLE TO PRODUCE IN STILL LARGER QUANTITIES.

TO DESTROY THIS FACTORY WOULD RESTRICT PRODUCTION OF FIGHTER PLANES.

THE FACTORY IS BUILT ALONG THE RAILWAY LINE BRISTOL-WICKWAR APPROX 2 KILOM NORTH OF DOUBLE JUNCTION OF WESTERLEIGH.

ADJOINING THE FACTORY THE RAILWAY LINE BRANCHES OFF TO N.W. (THORNBURY).

ASSEMBLY (SHOPS) AT FACTORY NEAR YATE AIRFIELD (10 284).

TRANSLATION OF GERMAN TEXT.

A translation into English of the above directive aimed at Luftwaffe pilots raiding Great Britain.

A panoramic aerial view of Parnall's at Yate, after the German raids of 27 February 1941 and Friday 7 March. The area just left of centre gives an idea of the extensive damage caused. Notice the close proximity of the main railway lines and sidings, the latter being well stocked with wagons. This was an LMS route over which the GWR had running powers.

The interior of Parnall's following the attack by a German bomber on 27 February 1941. An oil bomb hit the drawing office which became an inferno.

This outside view shows the entrance to the main office block at Parnall Aircraft Ltd, Yate, after being hit by high-explosive bombs.

The devastation of the main gun turret construction shop at Parnall's after the first German attack in which fifty employees lost their lives.

A view along the front of Parnall's following the Luftwaffe raid. Note the FN turrets in crates and on the ground by the lorry.

Responsible for the severe damage to Parnall's on both raids was a lone Heinkel He 111, similar to this He 111H-1 shot down at Dalkeith, repaired and flown in RAF markings as AW177.

A low-pass aerial shot of bomb-damaged Parnall's at Yate. Note the RAF Queen Mary articulated long wheelbase lorry in front of the wrecked office buildings.

The phoenix risen: an aerial view of the rebuilt Yate works of Parnall's in which gun turrets and parts for Lancaster and Lincoln bombers were built as well as a substantial number of Spitfire airframes. The old airfield is above and to right of the works.

The rebuilt main turret shop at Parnall's with FN 121 Avro Lancaster tail turrets under construction.

An Avro Lancaster tail turret (FN 121) minus its cupola. Notice the gunner's seat, the four .303in Browning machine-guns and the belt-fed ammunition.

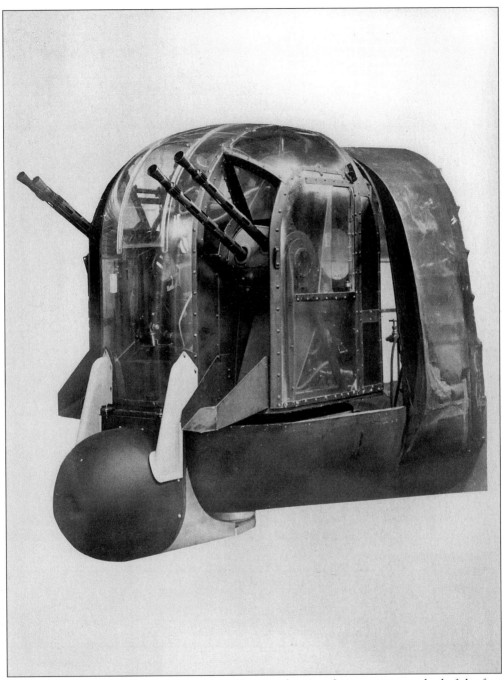

An exterior view of an FN 121 Lancaster tail turret showing the mounting method of the four Browning guns and an innovation on later Lancasters, a radar scanner/controller. This feature became standard on the Lancaster's successor, the Avro Lincoln.

An April 1945 scene with Lancaster rear fuselages under construction at Temple Cloud, on the Parnall Aircraft's satellite works.

With its Parnall-built turrets in evidence, this Avro Lancaster B.I (PA412/'KO-J') of 115 Squadron RAF is updated to Far East standard Mk I (FE).

Another April 1945 shot of Avro Lancaster D.4 rear fuselage main structure jigs with women workers at Parnall's Temple Cloud No. 1 factory (The Quarries).

In Parnall's No. 2 Factory at Temple Cloud was this Lancaster fin and rudder paint shop, shown here in April 1945.

The most famous extant Lancaster is PA474 *City of Lincoln*, of the Battle of Britain Memorial Flight, seen here landing at Fairford, Glos., on 12 July 1985, for the International Air Tattoo.

The fin structure of Lancasters and Lincolns was identical: this close-up shows the assembly of such a component at Parnall's Temple Cloud No. 2 factory.

With a modified fuselage, wing layout and uprated Merlin engines, the Lincoln succeeded Lancasters in service. This is RA638 featuring a number of Parnall-built components and turrets.

An Avro Lincoln B Mk 2 (RF385/'DX-G') from 57 Squadron RAF Bomber Command, with four 1,750hp Packard-built Merlin 68 engines. Note the modified nose in comparison to the Lancaster.

Once its Yate works had been rebuilt after the German bombing, Parnall Aircraft became a main sub-contractor for the production of Spitfire airframes. In this scene Spitfire wing leading edges are under construction with various types of jigs and trestles in use.

A famous outline of a remarkable aeroplane, the Supermarine Spitfire. Parnall's built numerous Spitfire airframe components for the type. This Spitfire Vb (R6923/'QJ-S') was from 92 Squadron.

A sight which many a Luftwaffe airman feared: a flight of Spitfires. These three are Mk Vbs from 243 Squadron, the nearest being EN821/'SN-M'.

Part of Parnall's sub-contract programme late in the war included components for the Gloster Meteor jet fighter. This shot shows an early Meteor F.1 (EE221) allocated to 616 Squadron Fighter Command.

Meteor F.1s, containing parts made by Parnall's at Yate, of 616 Squadron at Lübeck, Germany, in 1945. The nearest aircraft is EE219/'YQ-D'.

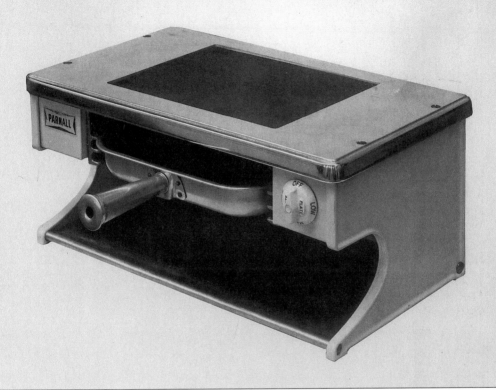

After the war Parnall Aircraft Ltd quickly severed connections with the aircraft industry and entered the field of domestic appliances such as cookers, washing machines, clothes presses etc. Here an early hotplate and grill is shown. Note the company name of Parnall embellishing the front left panel.

Acknowledgements

To compile a book whose content is mainly pictorial places much reliance on the co-operation of organizations, establishments and individuals to supply photographs and illustrations. It is, therefore, with sincere gratitude that I convey my thanks to the following, without whose help this book would have been a non-starter.

British Aerospace (Aircraft Group), Kingston-on-Thames and Filton; L. Callaway (ex-works manager at George Parnall & Co.); Ian Carnochan (ex-T.I. Jackson Ltd, Yate); Ted Chapman; the late Captain Frank T. Courtney; E. Draycott (ex-ground engineer and works inspector, George Parnall & Co.); Fleet Air Arm Museum; Mrs Margaret Fry (ex-George Parnall & Co.); Norman Hall-Warren (ex-design office, George Parnall & Co.); Eric Harlin; Imperial War Museum; the late A.J. Jackson; T.I. Jackson Ltd, Yate; Derek N. James; George Jenks (Avro Historical Research Group); John A. Long (Parnall & Sons Ltd); Mark Parnall of Cornwall; Brian Pickering ('MAP'); Richard Riding; Bruce Robertson; Rolls-Royce (aero-engine division), Bristol; Royal Aeronautical Society; Royal Aircraft Establishment (Main Library); RAF Museum; Brian Stainer (*Aviation Photo News*); Shell UK (aviation division); M.J. Tozer collection; Westland Helicopters Ltd.